A REASON TO LIVE

A REASON TO LIVE

Donalyn Powell

BETHANY HOUSE PUBLISHERS

MINNEAPOLIS, MINNESOTA 55438
A Division of Bethany Fellowship, Inc.

The names of people in this book have been changed to honor the confidence of those who dared to share their experiences with Donalyn Powell.

None of the models used for photographs are teenagers who have attempted suicide.

Photo on page 53 by Lori Mylander.
Photos on pages 30, 64, 68, 96, 104, 122, and 128 by Dick Easterday.

Copyright © 1989
Donalyn Powell
All Rights Reserved

Published by Bethany House Publishers
A Division of Bethany Fellowship, Inc.
6820 Auto Club Road, Minneapolis, Minnesota 55438

Printed in the United States of America

Library of Congress Cataloging-in-Publication Data

Powell, Donalyn.
    A reason to live / Donalyn Powell.
       p.   cm.

    1. Teenagers—United States—Suicidal behavior—Case studies.
I. Title.

HV6546.P68   1989
362.2'8'0835—dc20   89–37346
ISBN 1-55661-076-9   CIP

Dedicated

To my brothers

Lemont and Dan

DONALYN POWELL is an author/speaker who has worked as a freelance photographer and artist as well as a packaging development coordinator for an international cosmetic and fragrance company. The author of the recently published *Through a Child's Eyes,* she also serves as senior-high youth counselor in her church. She and her husband make their home in Lynchburg, Virginia.

Contents

Foreword

Donalyn lives on Sunny Lake Farm at the foothills of the Blue Ridge Mountains of Virginia. Her down-to-earth style makes her quite at home with her surroundings.

Being raised in a Christian home, with a desire to serve the Lord, led her to seek God's will for her life.

As a result, she has been serving the Lord for many years as a Sunday school teacher and youth counselor, because she was drawn to the needs of today's young people. She has also worked with teenagers on many levels outside of the church. This has given her the opportunity to understand their problems as *they* see them, and to share her faith in God. Working with teens who want to take their own life has given her an insight and ability to reach these young people that is rare and powerful.

After completing college with a degree in art, she was quickly recognized as an award-winning photographer and designer. Remembering her desire to serve the Lord, she dedicated her talents and her life to Him. Publishing her first book left no question as to how God was planning to use her.

When you meet this young lady, she captures you with a gracious smile radiating from an inner warmth. The energy she possesses flows in your direction and you are captivated by her presence. But the real depth and beauty of this young woman is her love for the Lord.

Watching her touch the hearts of those around her, you know she is trusting God. Each book she writes she gives to the Lord as a gift from willing hands and a thankful heart.

It is clear that she has been able to reach the heart-cry of the young people whose letters, stories, and thoughts appear on the pages of *this* book. In her usual warm and creative way, she has shown us *God's* reason to live.

Linda Beahm, M.D.
Family Practice

Acknowledgments

Anything requiring a great deal of work is usually done with the help of friends. There were several who believed in this book as strongly as I did, and contributed to the birth of these pages.

Ramona Tucker, my editor and friend, encouraged me daily with the words that will always rest in my heart: "I want you to write."

Jeff Tucker, my friend and Ramona's husband, understands the bond between a writer and editor and the endless hours they spend together.

Bob DeVaul and Jack Henly were always on call with photographic advice.

Annette Heinrick and CarolAnn Redmon spent long hours typing my manuscripts.

Silvana Faulkenberry gave graphic assistance.

And many teens modeled for the photographs used in this book.

Janice and Bob DeLong and Ralf and Lois Daisy are two special couples who have always remembered me in prayer.

My sister Joan, and Catherine Parker, whom I lovingly refer to as "Miss Catherine," have always been willing to lend a helping hand.

Dr. Michael Parker lifted me up through the times I carried the pain of these young people in my heart and added laughter when I'd take the time to play.

Mrs. Virginia Anderson, my very special Granny, always had dinner on the table so I could have more time to write.

Grandmother Countess Von Schenk, although many miles separate us, has been a constant source of inspiration for me.

Sharon Madison and David Hazard, my editors at Bethany House, encouraged and assisted me.

Dr. Linda Beahm spent many long hours gathering facts on teen suicide as well as sharing a personal account of one family's great loss.

And I can't forget about Mama—the wonderful love of Jesus was taught to me by my Christian mother, and it has carried me to where I am today.

As I finish this manuscript and read over the words, I see them as more than just words I have written, they are words He wrote through me. I owe everything to the Lord—especially the confident assurance to go on and on and on.

Donalyn

To my very special friends:

Teens who have written their heart-breaking stories and the parents who have shared the most difficult trial of their lives—learning to live without their child because of the tragedy of suicide.

Preface

His call came late one Sunday night. "Hello, is this Donalyn Powell?"

"Yes, it is."

"I overheard my father talking about you with someone on the plane coming home from Washington, D.C. I understand you're writing a book on teen suicide and that you're taking letters from teenagers who have tried to kill themselves. My name is John Reed, and I want to know if this is going to be confidential."

I assured him it would be, and he began his story.

It seemed as if he couldn't express what he wanted to say fast enough. I realized immediately he needed someone to just listen to him. Even though his thoughts were all about suicide, deep within him was a driving desire to find someone who could give him a reason to live.

"I tried to kill myself last year, and I just tried to kill myself again, but we can't tell anyone because of the high position my father holds."

I wondered what would happen if he gave his father the chance to understand the pain he was going through. The last words from this young man I could not see shared the true emptiness of his pain: "I don't even know who I am."

As I entered the room, I found myself looking into the fear-filled eyes of Claire, a beautiful sixteen-year-old girl. She hadn't answered my knock, but I'd entered anyway. At first she wouldn't talk. I could only sit by her and recall her recent past.

Claire had no desire to be part of the world that existed beyond the four walls of her bedroom, but she'd run out of excuses to stay home from school. Others had noticed her withdrawal, but felt it was just a temporary reaction to the recent break-up with her boyfriend Scott. There was much more.

It had been only a year since her parents had fought through a painful divorce. Claire had grown tired of feeling as if she were the only means of communication between them. She was torn by her love for both of them.

Claire had been friends with Scott for a long time. They'd grown up in the same neighborhood, gone to the same school, and attended the same church. They began dating only weeks after her parents had announced they were getting a divorce. His parents had divorced several years earlier, so he was able to understand what she was going through. She turned to him for the attention and affection she didn't feel she was getting at home.

Their relationship progressed physically further than either had expected. Claire knew she was too young to get married, but she had become emotionally and physically dependent on Scott.

When Scott began to feel the pressure of their relationship—and the responsibility for helping her get through her parents' divorce—he unexpectedly announced that they were too young to be so involved.

His short and cold explanation made her feel used and ashamed of being physically involved with him. Her loneliness, guilt, and rejection were more than she could bear.

It was only days ago that she had been forced to leave her room and return to school—and on that same afternoon she had tried to take her own life. Now, suddenly, she turned and hugged me. Her tears were wet against my shoulder, and in her broken voice she whispered, "I'm so tired of hurting."

———

Last summer I found myself surrounded by deeply moving stories of young people who had taken their own lives. The first story of suicide left me in shock. When it was followed by another, I wondered and feared who would be next. I could feel the hurt and lostness of these victims.

And then there were those close to the victims—in some cases the wounds never heal. Some feel forever guilty, wondering what they could have done to prevent an unnecessary death.

I tried to put each tragic story out of my thoughts and think of "brighter" things.

But each time I did, another hurting youth would find his way into my life. I was overwhelmed. I could understand what each one was feeling and it forced me to relive the pain of my own past.

When I turned nineteen, I began an eight-year battle with illness. Operations and hospital visits stole the joy from life and made me question my own reason for existing. Some days I would have to fight *hard* for my own life. Other days the pain I felt was stronger than my own desire to live. I prayed, begging God to let me die. I would sit in church, looking at the cross in prayer, asking the Lord over and over what I'd done that I had to live like this. When would it all end? Hiding my pain, I would wipe my tears so neither Mama nor anyone else could see, but I continued to feel that for me there was no way out.

Even as a Christian, I felt death was the answer to all my problems. I would keep my Bible by my bed, and each night I'd read verses that told me what it would be like in heaven with God. I'd have a new body that would never be sick again. But suicide was *my* answer, not God's.

I know now that if I *had* committed suicide then, I would have missed the future God had planned for me. Through all those years of not understanding why I hurt, God was molding me with His loving hands.

Loving God doesn't free us from pain or disappointment, but it allows us to have the assurance that He will go through all our trials with us. I know that God used my pain to do His work in me. I also learned to cast even my biggest heartaches on the Lord, and I found that His shoulders are stronger than mine. I discovered that He loves me more than I ever had imagined.

I have a special prayer, which came out of that time—"Lord, wrap your arms around me so that I can feel your loving presence in my life today." Those simple words, and the trust that goes with them, have carried me through so many tough days. But then, God is *always* there to carry us through when we call on His name.

In God's time for me, I began to understand. I moved from hopelessness to hope, from questions to understanding, from lost dreams to building new ones. And instead of taking my own life, I asked God to help me accept His reasons for why I should live.

Today, each time I hear the heart-breaking story of a young person who has tried to commit suicide or sad account of a parent or friend of one who succeeded in killing himself, I feel a sense of responsibility to convince them suicide is not the answer.

But I quickly realize that there is nothing I can do or say on my own. God's love and strength are their hope. They need to believe that He can heal every broken heart and know that He is with us every day of our lives, giving us the courage to live.

If you have attempted suicide, if you have thought about killing yourself, or if you are close to someone who has, I ask you to give me the next few hours. Put your hand in mine and let me share with you the stories, the pain, and the promises of hope from other young people so much like yourself. Walk with me and believe, as I do, that when we are forced to face unbearable pain and disappointment, something bigger, brighter, and better can arise from the ashes of every hurt.

I have learned that the greatest secret to a rich, full, happy life is to seek and find God's plan for me with each sunrise. Each time the stars come out again, I want to be able to say, "I've done the best I could with what God gave me—His life for mine!"

Suicide is *not* the answer, God's *life* in you is.

Donalyn

Are You Listening, Or Running?

One of the most important lessons I've ever learned came when I was lost and afraid. I wasn't lost in a strange city or the deep woods—I was lost *inside*. I didn't know where I was or how I got there. I prayed and prayed, but I couldn't see a way out to the happy, fun-filled life others seemed to be living. I was tired and I didn't really want to quit—but I couldn't go on anymore.

When I finally stopped long enough to listen, the Lord began to teach me an important lesson. I'd been so busy thinking about *myself* and my own answers, that if the Lord *had* tried to answer my prayer, I couldn't have even heard Him.

There *are* solutions to every problem. Giving up isn't one of them. God's answers are not always the same as ours though. He may have another path He wants us to follow. But we will never know His reason to live if we don't *pray, wait* and *listen*.

1

Suicide Is Forever

Dear Donalyn,

There's one day I'll never be able to forget.

I just got home from school when the phone started ringing. It was a friend, telling me David had committed suicide.

I told her, "I don't believe you!" But I was already crying when I asked her to repeat what she said. I pressed my hands against my head, trying to stop the words that came back so loudly. "David is dead."

All I could do was scream, "*No*. I don't understand! I just don't understand! I just don't understand!"

I called Mom, but she couldn't leave work. I ran to my room and began to throw everything around. I couldn't stop crying. I thought I'd done something wrong.

When Mom got home she just held me. I told her it was all my fault. David had asked me not to go away that weekend with her and the rest of the family. He wanted me to stay in town so we could go out together.

David had a lot of problems. He and his brother Tony were only nine months apart in age and they used to do everything together. Less than a year ago, Tony was killed in a motorcycle accident. It seemed like David wouldn't let go of Tony's death.

The last thing David said to me was, "I'll call you Monday morning."

That night I cried myself to sleep. The next morning I went to school because if I stayed home I'd just go crazy. My friends gave me hugs and told me they were sorry.

I couldn't go to David's house. I saw his mom at the funeral home. She gave me a hug and told me the last few days of his life were happy because he'd spent them with me.

David had left his mom a letter, saying he hoped everyone would understand. He said he couldn't live without his brother. David's mom just kept saying they couldn't live without each other. She buried David next to Tony with a marker that says, "Forever Together."

After David's funeral, I kept going over the last week we were together. David had never given me any clues. He was depressed because, a few days earlier, it was Tony's birthday. I thought about our last date together and our last kiss. That night David seemed to be feeling better. I thought about never having the chance to say goodbye again.

I found out through a close friend of ours that David was going to give me his class ring on Monday. All I could think about was that I never told him how much I cared for him. Why did this have to happen?

David used to talk about being in the Olympics. He was a great runner and his room was full of trophies. At first, I talked about David 24 hours a day. Then some of my friends said something to me about it, and I began to feel like I was getting on everyone's nerves. I don't talk about David anymore. I don't like to go places where we used to go together. There are too many memories.

When I think about David now, I don't think he really meant to do it. Sometimes I get depressed because I'd love to see him. I'll always want to know how long we would have lasted because we were so good together.

I'm dating someone else now, and I really like him. But I'm afraid to care about him because if something happens to him I don't want to go through the same thing again.

There's a movie that I really love. This guy dies, but he comes back to see this girl that he loved just one last time. I'd give anything if that could be me.

Lisa

W hy didn't he tell us?"
"I don't know, I guess he
    couldn't."
"If we could only have a second
    chance."
"Suicide doesn't give second
    chances."

Dear Lisa,

I want you always to remember that you are *not* responsible for what someone else does with their life. Your searching heart was looking for the answer to David's death, but blaming yourself is not that answer.

You need to let go of your feelings of guilt and realize that David was responsible for his own actions. He'd been upset over his brother's death for a long time, and you had nothing to do with David committing suicide. At the time you left to go away with your parents, David may not even have been thinking about taking his own life. Since you weren't there, you don't even know the final events that took place before he died.

David knew how you felt about him, or he wouldn't have planned to give you his class ring. So you really did tell David that you cared about him—even if you didn't say it with words.

Lisa, we all need to communicate our feelings with someone who'll listen. When David first died it was a shock for you and everyone else involved. All you could think about was David. It was only natural that you talked about him so much. When your friends brought it to your attention, they didn't mean that you could never bring up his name again. Because they cared about you, they probably didn't want to see you hurt anymore. And maybe they thought that *not* talking about him would make it hurt less.

Don't assume that if you begin to care about someone else that you will lose them, too. The time you and David spent together was good, and good memories are wonderful. You need to find a place to rest those memories in your heart and go on with your life.

I think you're right about David not wanting to die. He wanted a way out from hurting so much, and he didn't know what else to do. David didn't realize that pain goes away, but suicide is forever.

I wish I could tell you there wouldn't be any more hurts or unanswered questions in your life. But I have had to bring many unanswered questions to God. And, through my tears, I wondered if I'd ever stop hurting. I *did* stop hurting, and I began to understand the work of God's hand in my life. Now I know that God was with me all along.

When I was growing up, my parents moved around a lot. I often attended more than one school in one year. I often wished I had one home to grow up in and one town full of friends where I would never say goodbye.

As we grow up, we're building new dreams every day. Some of those dreams can come true, but some will never become a reality. When I lose a dream, I turn to the Lord and ask Him to put His desires in my heart. I know that the Lord has something good in store for me because He knows all about dreams. He also knows what's best for each one of us, so we need to trust Him.

The truth is, His dream for your life—even if you experience pain—will be the *best* dream of all.

One day at a time, I'm placing my life in God's hands.

I will lift my head high in His
    direction
as I bring Him my
disappointments,
broken dreams
and
unanswered questions.
In His strength I can stand tall,
because God's timing is better
    than mine.
In God's time
I will better understand
all His plans for my life.
And I'll be thankful.
I take all my tomorrows and
    place them in God's hands.

31

2

A God of Second Chances

Mrs. Pate asked me to follow her down the hall. There was a confident assurance in the sound of her footsteps. When we walked into her office, I sat in the chair across from her desk. It wasn't until that moment that we really had a chance to look each other in the face.

She was an attractive woman, perhaps in her early forties. Her brown, short hair softly framed her face. She had eyes that were warm and friendly, making me feel comfortable in her presence. They showed no sign of the hardship I had heard she'd just gone through.

At the same time I was checking her out, I could sense she was not only looking *at* me, but *inside* me.

And then, the heartache appeared on her face as a deep sigh opened up the door of her heart. She allowed me to enter, breaking the silence between us as she placed the past few years of her son's life in my hands.

"There are many sides to hurting. You would never have thought something like this could happen in a town with only a post office, a grocery store, and a garage. But it did."

She went on to explain that it all seemed to begin with Brad's car accident. He was sixteen and going through a "show-off" stage. Once, driving too fast, he had a terrible accident that left him with 300 stitches in his head.

"While Brad was still in the hospital, he began saying

32

he couldn't remember anything. The doctor assured us that nothing was wrong with him. But he kept telling us he had a hard time remembering.

"When he went back to school, his old friends made fun of him. It wasn't long before I noticed he was making new friends. But I thought, in time, things would be back to normal. I didn't know that those friends accepted him on one term only—anyone who got high with them was 'okay.'

"Soon he was forging checks and stealing things out of the house to get the money he needed to support his drug habit. Lying became a daily routine. His grades dropped. When he quit school, his father and I weren't surprised.

"As Brad drifted further and further from us, he seemed lost and haunted. Looking for a way to help him, we sent him to a drug rehab center. But their idea of "help" was just to give him legal drugs.

"When he came back home we weren't prepared for his newest means to get the drugs he wanted. Although he was only 16, the state police began to slip him money, which he used for drugs. They used him as an undercover narcotics agent. We knew something strange was going on. So one night we followed him and forced him to tell us the truth. We stood at a pay phone as he called his partner at the police station. We were outraged that the state police used a young boy as a means to make their drug busts. The police warned us that if we went public with what they were doing, the drug pushers would have Brad killed.

"But when the police could no longer support his addiction, our son turned back to robbing. When he was caught stealing cars, I warned him that if he stole another car he couldn't come back home. In the time he took to laugh at my warning, he stole another car.

"I should have known I wasn't talking to my son," she said, her eyes filling with tears, "but only to the shell of a human being. His 'food' consisted of drugs of only the highest quality—coke, heroin, acid. His only thought was, *How can I get my next fix?*

"What happened to the son I once knew?" Mrs. Pate pleaded. "The one who had a bright awareness in his eyes. The one who loved life. The son I miss and would give anything to hold again. Brad didn't just *live* life, he *experienced* it. Sure he had a strong will, but he also had compassion for others. He had a way about him that always melted my heart.

"Knowing these qualities were still alive somewhere inside Brad—and that we loved him—my husband and I sold our home to raise the money we needed to help him get rid of his craving for drugs. Still, we began to feel as though we'd failed him in some way—but we didn't know how. We felt guilty, and so helpless.

"Brad tried to kill himself. Not once, but several times. When a serious attempt to overdose failed, he told us, 'If I can't kill myself, I can *have* it done by someone else.' So he set up an armed robbery. When the police surrounded him, he walked out without taking anything, hoping they would shoot him. But they didn't—they took him to jail.

"Something inside of me still said, *Don't give up on him.* When I went to jail to see him, he was going through withdrawal. I cried and put my hands against the glass wall that separated us. He told me he loved me more than I'll ever know—but I should give up and let him die. When I left the jail that afternoon, I knew there was only one answer—God.

"This nightmare had been going on for two and a half years. If God had kept my son alive this long, I knew He had something special planned for his life. I believed

God would answer my prayer to save Brad's life.

"Then a minister started coming to the jail. He continued to tell Brad, day after day, about God's love. He said God had the healing power to help him put away his drug addiction for the rest of his life. One night, Brad called me. He was reading a Bible. He said he'd accepted Christ, and that he was ready to accept his legal punishment. At 19, he was facing sixty years in jail.

"But you know, a strange thing happened. While he prepared for his trial, a doctor's examination revealed that the car accident did affect Brad's thinking and reasoning ability. Brad felt as if a huge burden had been lifted from his shoulders. *Finally,* someone believed him.

"The more I went to jail to see him, the more I believed he was sincere in accepting Christ. He wasn't trying to live by his own wits anymore. He was depending on God's help.

"Before Brad's trial, we read from God's Word: 'You are prisoners of sin, every one of you. And prisoners don't have rights, but Jesus has every right there is! So if Jesus sets you free you will indeed be free.' (See John 8:34–36.)

"When God gave Brad a new birth, I knew that whatever we had to face, we would make it. Brad was sentenced to just one year! Today, he's out of jail and he's trying hard to be the young man God wants him to be. He's thankful to be alive, and that God gave Him another chance at life.

"To be honest," Mrs. Pate confided, "I almost threw away my relationship with God because of the pain we were going through. But instead I turned my life *toward* God. And He's used our pain to reach out to others who have gone through the same heartaches."

When I looked at my watch, *four hours* had quickly passed. She'd taken me into the most private areas of her life. My heart had ached as I'd watched her cry.

And now, with a special glow in her eyes, she said, "Today I can understand how God's hand was working in our lives. And I can only thank Him for being a God of second chances."

She finished, and I got up to hug her as we said goodbye. And I silently thanked God for the amazing way He works, even in the most difficult times of our lives.

Looking for a way out,
I took a chance on getting high.
But it didn't change a thing.
There are no perfect people and
    no perfect places
even when you are stoned.
Getting high all the time
ended up being a lot of trash.
And the places it takes you—
you don't want to go.

3

Something Worth Living For

I never thought I'd make it through those roller-coaster years. One day I'd feel like everything was all right, and the next day I'd feel like my whole world was caving in. I had a hard time dealing with my own anger. I'd be angry at the world because I didn't think life was fair. And I would be angry at myself if I felt like I wasn't good enough. I found myself trapped in a whirlwind of confusing notions, spiraling downward.

One day my anger turned on me. I tried to take my own life. At the time, I thought, "If I die then all my problems will be solved." But I really didn't think about being *dead*.

I wish someone had brought me here, to this cemetery. I think it would have made me feel like there had to be a better way than giving up and dying. I can't say graveyards make me feel good. I've never seen anyone singing as they left a funeral.

One day someone cared enough to tell me about Jesus and how He loved me so much that He died on the cross so I could have life. I started praying about everything. I even asked Him to help show me how to control my anger. I don't have all the answers, but prayer changed my life.

I still have a lot of growing up to do, but I know I can make it with Jesus in my life. I want to leave this world with people saying something more about me than, "He's the guy who killed himself."

4

Reaching for God

Dear Donalyn,

I felt like I was a complete failure. I couldn't sleep or eat or study for days. Everything was wrong, and there was a haze over my mind so that I couldn't come up with a plan to make things right.

I was ashamed of so many things. I had done something I knew was wrong, and I felt really guilty. But there was no one to talk to about it who would understand. No one to say the words I wanted to hear, "You're forgiven. Your whole future doesn't have to be ruined." I felt completely out of control. I tried hard to cover up my feelings of guilt and depression, but that didn't help. Sometimes I would end up crying in the stairwell between classes, then try to touch up my makeup and get to my next class only to sit in the back of class with a fake smile.

Finally, my mind rebelled along with my heart. I'd always been a top student. Now I just looked helplessly at my books. I couldn't concentrate enough to study. All I could think of was my problems, causing my grades to crash. Friends tried to help, knowing these grades were very important to my college plans. They sat for hours trying to study with me, but it seemed nothing was sinking in.

Then came the test that could make the difference between a really good college and a so-so school. Trying to answer questions was hopeless—my mind had gone blank. I finally surrendered my answer booklet, then went outside to wait for the results.

I saw all my future plans crumble when they told me, "You didn't pass."

I had to get far away. I felt like I'd failed at everything that was important to me, and I couldn't stand the pain of it all any longer. I drove for hours and finally ended up in a crowded parking lot. I was sure that no one would notice my little car until it was too late. I laid down on the back seat with a soda and a bag of pills. I'd carefully researched which combination of pills to take, so I would *not* be a failure at suicide, too. But instead of taking them, I just laid there for hours, crying. Finally, I fell asleep from exhaustion.

When I woke up, I began sipping the soda. I looked out at the stars. For the first time, the universe seemed to unfold in perfect order and sequence for me. I began to remember lessons I'd learned in Sunday school when I was little. God created the universe. He created me, and maybe He did have a plan for my life.

At first, I was reluctant to believe. Then, just a little, I realized that God was my Father and truly cares for me. I felt a growing sense of wonder at the vast power of God's control over stars and space and time. I felt humbled at the thought that God—the Creator of these stars and planets—looked down on one small planet, at one small person—me—and cared.

I threw away the bag of pills.

Thanks for listening,
Kathy

There's Nothing Broken He Can't Repair

Those broken baskets look like
my life."
"When I first looked, I didn't see
the broken parts because the
grass was hiding them."
"Those baskets can still be used
if someone would repair
them. It makes me think
about how Jesus repairs and
replaces our broken pieces so
we can go on to be everything
He wants us to be."

Dear Kathy,

I'm so glad you discovered on your own that you didn't need the bag of pills.

After all, who said you were a complete failure? Just you. The words we allow into our minds can do one of two things: drown us in our own self-pity, or encourage us to make it through the tough times. Sometimes we aren't even aware of the language that surrounds our lives. Have you listened to a song and liked the beat of the music—but when you stopped to really listen to the words, they brought you down?

I'm not surprised you failed your exam. You said yourself you couldn't focus enough to study. But *you tried*. That's what's important. Failing an exam isn't the end of the world. At least you know why you failed. It's a lot easier to make a change when you know why something happened. When we make mistakes and know why they happened, we can work harder to keep them from happening again. The grade isn't as important as being able to say, "I really did my best."

Often when we feel ashamed of something we've done, we build a wall that keeps everyone out—even the Lord. Something inside says, *I can't talk about what's wrong*. So what do we do? We hide and refuse to let anyone get close to us. We don't want anyone to touch us when we hurt.

One afternoon my younger brother fell off his bike. When my parents reached him, they knew he needed to go to the hospital—the cut on his leg was very deep. The last thing my brother wanted was to go to the hospital. He kept crying, "Mom, make the pain go away!" My parents explained that if they left his leg to heal on its own, it would have a bad scar. But if they took him to the hospital, the doctors could help his wound to heal properly. They'd give him the special care he needed and make the pain go away. His wound would heal much faster.

Just like my brother needed a doctor to take care of his leg, we need to let Jesus take care of our inner wounds. It's important to remember that He already sees our whole situation *and* the solution.

Kathy, after you realized you had done something wrong, you immediately put up a barrier to shield yourself from the hurt and the guilt of that sin, instead of bringing it before Jesus and confessing it, and asking Him to cleanse you and give you the strength you need to go on. This may seem like the hardest thing to do—admitting that you're wrong—but in the end you will walk away a clean and forgiven child of God, and that sure beats struggling in sin and guilt.

We can't always forget our mistakes. But we can learn from them and accept God's forgiveness. And then we're on the way to forgiving ourselves.

When I feel like I've really messed up, and I'm feeling guilty and hurt, I go through these steps: First, I begin to share everything I'm feeling with the Lord, and confess the things I've done wrong. Every little detail. Second, I thank God for loving me and sending His Son, Jesus, so that I can be forgiven and have eternal life. I thank Him that nothing can take that away from me. Third, I take some words from my heart and put them to music.

I wrote this little poem once:

Walk by my side
in all I do
so if I fall
I can reach for you.

I kept singing these words, like a song, over and over again. And guess what? The next morning I felt better.

49

In fact, most of the time the system works so well that I fall asleep before I ever get to step number four: Tell God what you're thankful for. The Lord cares so much for you and me. Although we make mistakes and disappoint Him, we can know His forgiveness and strength.

And we can also know his blessings.

It's Your Move

Watch that move!"

"What move?"

"The most important move
you'll ever make. The one
right after you feel like you've
really messed up your life."

"What are you talking about?"

"You can move in the direction
of Jesus. His love mends the
hurts. As you pray and listen,
He'll direct your steps. Or
you can let guilt slide in and
tell you that you're a failure.
You can move away from
Jesus and shut Him out,
along with everyone else.
That's when you can lose
your will to live."

"Why would anyone do *that?*"

"Because the pain we feel is so
strong sometimes it covers up
any other feelings of love and
understanding. But we
should never forget God
understands every hurt we
bring to Him, even when we

don't get the words right.
There are no limits on God's
love, His forgiveness, or His
plan to make us everything
He wants us to be. That's
why Jesus said, 'I'll never
leave you.' "

5

Someone to Walk With Us

Dear Donalyn,

I was born with a blood disease that's kept me in and out of hospitals all my life. My parents are good to me, but I've always felt like a burden to my whole family.

Dad works hard so there'll be money for my medication and treatments. The bills are heavy-duty. Mom stays home so she'll be around if I need her. My brothers are terrific—they stop by my room after school and tell me about their day and what's going on with my friends. But they're also a constant reminder that I'm not like them. While they're working out for football season, my "work-out" is another boring walk up and down a hospital hallway. They make plans with their girlfriends, but I wonder if I'll ever even have a date.

I'm 16 now. I've watched my family rearrange their lives for me. They've given up so much. And there's nothing I can give *them*. I can't even promise to get well enough one day to plan a vacation and know for sure I can go. I don't know if I'll *ever* get well. I can't stand the way I'm ruining their lives.

I go through periods of remission that can last a couple of months. I feel much stronger and I can do some of the things I really enjoy, like riding my bike and roller skating. I even go to school and go out for pizza with my friends. I feel like I'm alive. When I'm feeling good I want to do everything I can, because I don't know how long it will last. When I least expect it, my strength leaves. I'm left with only a memory of what it felt like to be like my brothers. *Normal.*

It's hard to begin to feel like a real person—like an average guy—and then have it all taken away from you. Mom always tells me one day I'll be well. I ask her when that day will come. She can't tell me. Sometimes I pretend that I'm someone else and that I can do all the things I dream of. For a while I feel better. But something always happens to remind me of who I really am.

A couple weeks ago, Mom went out for a few hours. While she was gone I took an overdose of my medication. I was so tired; I just wanted to die. But my attempt only landed me in the hospital again, and afterward I felt like I was a *greater* burden on my family. Mom blamed herself and said it was her fault because she left me alone. I didn't try to kill myself to hurt her! I'm just so sick of living this way.

I see two worlds. In one, everyone is healthy and alive and your dreams come true. But the other? It's my world— a world where I'm just a burden to everyone. I don't want to live in my world anymore. Please tell me how I can live in my brothers' world.

Tommy

What's Your Name?

I'm all alone."
"No you're not!"
"But I feel all alone."
"That's only because you want
    to feel alone."
"Then *you* tell me where is
    everybody when I need
    them?"
"*I'm* here."
"What's your name?"
"Jesus."

Dear Tommy,

I can understand how you feel—alone in your private world. None of us wants to deal with being sick and feeling helpless. But *walling* yourself in your own world will only keep you from feeling as though your life isn't as worthwhile as your brothers'. We all live in the *same* world—the one God created—but we experience life differently. That's what makes us unique.

I think you know how much your family loves you. Remember that you're the only one who can separate yourself from them. Everyone has a special place inside himself where he can run and hide when he's hurting. But there's a danger of wanting to stay there forever. And you know what? I've never known a burden that gets better when you stuff it inside. Your family may not always understand—they're not walking in your tennis shoes. It's up to you to let them know how you feel.

There *is* hope. No matter what we face, for however long we live, someone will walk with us. *Jesus.* All of us have had at least one dream that will never come true because it requires us to change something we have no power to change. And it really does hurt to want something so bad, when deep in your heart you know it will never come true.

Tommy, I want you to know something. I understand your pain because I spent eight years in and out of hospitals, too. At that time I couldn't understand what purpose God could ever have for my life. Just like you, I got tired. Sick of the whole thing. Every time I faced another needle or thermometer or operation I wanted to die. I'd ask the Lord if I could be in heaven with Him. When we are tired, our bodies and our minds are the most vulnerable.

I can't tell you how many nights my mom sat by my bed and told me, "When God takes something away, he gives you something else in return." I wondered what God would give me. You wondered if you would ever have a date. Girls often daydream about whom they'll fall in love with and marry one day. I wondered if a guy would ever care for a girl like me. By the time I was nineteen I questioned if I would ever get well, and I already knew that I could never have a child.

But I had a very special dream. I wanted to be an artist and a writer. Many people encouraged me to do something with the talents God gave me; I always had an excuse that never took my work farther than my bedroom.

One night I had a dream that I died and went to heaven. My hands were empty, I had nothing to offer Him. I met the Lord, and He asked me, "What did you do with everything I gave you?"

That dream haunted me for a long time. I knew that I didn't want to meet the Lord empty-handed. I'd spent years telling myself that I wasn't worth much. What could I possibly have to give? In my eyes, I found no purpose for my life, because I'd forgotten what I was worth to God.

What He began to teach me I'll never forget. For the next several weeks, everything I heard seemed to have something to do with what we are worth as a person. I saw television shows about young people who couldn't walk but accomplished outstanding goals. I heard sermons about how much we're treasured by God. I was reminded that my life was worth Jesus dying on the cross. Then I heard someone say, "Everyone says it's so hard to get started. But all you have to do is begin." How could I begin?

I was the only one who could change. But things didn't start to change until I asked the Lord to help me know what it was He wanted me to do with my life. I should have known His answer. With an open heart, I listened to His Word by reading my Bible. I knew He wanted me to love Him above everything else, so that He could direct my life and prepare me for what He wanted me to do—even when I didn't think I could do or give *anything* worthwhile.

The Lord had grabbed my attention! I finally let go of some of the dreams I knew could never come true. I stopped reminding myself of what I *couldn't* do and I began to focus on what I *could* do.

One night, I announced to my family that I was going to go to college. This was a big surprise for everyone.

I went out and enrolled in a local college as an art student. I started out taking one class, and when I saw that I could complete one class I took another. It wasn't long before I became a full-time student. I started by setting one goal and reaching it one step at a time. There were times when I had to drop a class because of my illness, but I always went back and picked up where I left off. I was older than most of the other students, and even though it was difficult, I never quit. *I graduated.* Starting with one small goal led me to accomplish a greater goal.

During those years I finally did get well. Sometimes I feel guilty when I think of the days I wasted. But the Lord reminds me of the lessons I've learned, and I thank Him for bringing me this far.

In my heart I continued to feel that the Lord wanted me to give my talents to Him. I knew I wanted to be a writer, so I plunged into my art and my writing. I gave my first book to the Lord and I knew that if this was what He wanted from me He would open a door. With a trembling heart, I sent my manuscript to a publisher. The Lord blessed that timid step, and it was accepted for publication! Finally, I knew something of what the Lord was giving me in return.

Tommy, the Lord also has a job for *you* to do. No one else can do it. It could be related to something you are involved with right now. Think about setting a small goal, and perhaps it can lead you to accomplish an even greater goal. *Trust God*—even when you can't imagine what purpose He has for you life. I know, because He used me when I thought, like you, that I had nothing to give.

The Nicest Thing
About You Is. . . .

I used to worry about looking
   funny
and having people stare at me
   all day long.
I've even asked myself, "What
   am I doing here?"
Sure, I'm different.
But if God wanted me like
   everybody else,
He would have made me that
   way.
And besides, I've got a great
   personality.

Go ahead. We've all felt
    rejection
sometime in our lives.
A smile and a few more steps
    will get you in."
"But what if it doesn't? What if
    they don't
like me?"
"You're never a failure when
    you try.
Anyway, it's hard to turn down
    a smile."

6

Open Arms

Dear Donalyn,

I wasn't happy. I wasn't *anything*. I used to be real wild and do things that I don't even want to talk about now. The friends I used to hang around with would have wild parties, and all of us had sex with the guys we liked. I was raised in a home where we went to church. But there wasn't very much talk about the kind of life God wanted us to lead.

My parents got a divorce last year, and I really started to get confused about what was right and wrong. Mom was so busy working after Dad left, she didn't keep up with what my older sister and I were doing. My sister got involved with drugs, and I really didn't care about who I went with. I felt so lost. I'd pray, but it didn't change me. My sister was stoned most of the time, and I started to feel like I had to look after her. So I stopped running around with my friends as much as I used to. The crazy thing about all of this was our parents didn't even notice.

One night, when I was changing the channels on my radio, I heard a girl talking about drugs. I kept it there and found out she'd been a prostitute and a drug addict. Then one day, someone told her about Jesus and that He wouldn't give up on her. He told her that Jesus would love her in a way that would fill all her needs and give her the strength to give up dope, and also the confidence in herself to find a job. She accepted the Lord, and she's married now and a mother.

In the past when I listened to Christian radio stations I laughed at some of the preachers—but now I couldn't learn enough about Jesus. One night, I heard a sermon about knowing you're saved. I started crying, and I knew what Jesus was trying to tell me. I accepted Jesus as my personal Savior that night. I asked Him to live in my heart and take charge of my life.

It wasn't easy for me going to school and seeing my friends. They knew I was different, but they still wanted me to do some of the things I used to do with them. But I didn't. I also thought I could talk to my family about Jesus, but they really didn't want to hear it. My boyfriend really didn't understand either. I told him that Jesus had changed my life, and I wanted to start doing what was right for me. I still wanted to see him, but I didn't want us to have sex anymore. For the first time in my life, I felt clean.

But then my sister told me I needed help, and I watched my friends walk out of my life. The boyfriend I didn't think I could live without broke up with me.

The more I read my Bible, the more I wanted to be with Jesus. I felt all alone, and I cried and prayed. I couldn't go on any longer. I thought it would be better to be in heaven with Jesus than here on earth. So I cut my wrists and lay down on my bed. I woke up later in a hospital bed. My sister told me she found me just in time to save my life. My first thought was, *Why didn't she let me die?*

After I got home, I had a lot of time to think about what I'd done. I still felt alone, but I realized the Lord didn't want me to die. Sometimes I get scared because I wonder if I'll ever try it again.

Love,
Heather

Choose friends who have the
    qualities
of love
and happiness
because those things are
    contagious.

Dear Heather,

When we're unhappy, it keeps us from feeling all the good things in life. It makes us forget that we can have good feelings inside us again, that those good feelings are within our grasp—if we choose to reach for them. Being unhappy for a long time is a real downer. It can keep you from seeing bright tomorrows or feeling strong enough to try hard at anything you do.

When you go through problems and keep falling down, you need to share with someone you trust and respect. Do you have a friend like that? If you don't feel comfortable sharing with someone your own age, talk to a professional counselor. Seeking help doesn't mean you're weird or anything like that. It means something is *right*; you're growing as a person and you care enough about yourself to say, "I need someone to help me."

I want you to remember something else: There's one counselor who's always there for you. And when you ask Him to help, no problem is too big or too small, because He cares about every detail of your life. Jesus' tender mercy and lovingkindness is eternal. He has unfailing love for everyone who calls upon His name.

We often forget God waits for us with open arms. On days when I feel alone, I ask the Lord to wrap His arms around me so that I can feel His love. I once learned that when I bring my needs to the Lord in the morning, then He stays with me all through the day. When I ask for help, He always answers my prayers and wraps me up with so much love that I'm bursting with it. I can *feel* the joy that comes with the love of our Lord. Guess what happens next? This love gives you an inner confidence so that you can believe in yourself and get through whatever you're facing.

He'll do all this for you, too, when you pray and ask for His help.

Now that doesn't mean that everything will turn out the way *we* want.

In your mind, it was right for your parents to stay together. When you love your parents it's hard to understand why they can't love each other. I believe that every parent who is going through a divorce would do anything to keep their child from hurting. But their own hurt is so strong they don't know *how* to keep you from hurting.

But even what we *know* is right doesn't always happen. At this point, I'll bet it appears that nothing lasts forever, so doing what seems right doesn't seem to matter that much anymore. These are the times we need to pray for our families, as we ask God to help us accept and understand the decisions of others, especially the ones that affect our lives. When we put our faith in others we will always be disappointed. People aren't perfect so they continue to make mistakes. That's why we should *pray* for those we love, but *look* to God and His truths as our perfect example.

Heather, when you wanted someone—a *person*—to care for you, your boyfriend was wrapped up in the addiction of sex. That sounds cold and uncaring, but sex can be just as strong an addiction as a drug. An immature sexual relationship has little concern for one's deep personal feelings or beliefs. The freedom to be yourself in the relationship is lost. You feel as though you're tied up, in an emotional cage. You thought you would feel loved, but instead you still feel incomplete.

When God told us to wait for sex until marriage, it wasn't because He wanted to hurt us. It was because He wanted to keep us from *being* hurt. Today, young people across the world are learning in some pretty sad ways about the dangers of sex outside of marriage.

As we grow up, each of us is confronted with a very important question: "What kind of life am I going to live?"

No one else is responsible for how *you* answer that question—for how you live. Only you are.

71

But the fact of the matter is, you can *want* to do the right thing and keep failing. Your behavior won't change until you change the desires in your heart. And how do you do that? By asking the Lord to come into your life. Through your love for Jesus, your desire will be to become the kind of young man or woman He wants you to be.

The night you accepted Jesus as your personal Savior, Heather, you took the first step. And as you grow in the Lord, you'll better understand everything that God is and will be in your life.

Breaking up with a boyfriend who didn't understand where you're coming from is a smart move. God also understands your need for friendships. Pray that He'll bring Christian friends into your life, ones who'll help you grow in the Lord.

Feeling clean for the first time in your life was God's grace and forgiveness. After what you've been through, you now know God's cleansing and His love. Let that be your strength in standing up to temptations. Each day you'll grow stronger in the Lord, and what's right will seem important again. The respect for yourself and what you want out of life will be so clear that decisions won't be as hard to make.

God doesn't want you to dwell on the problems of the past. He wants you to make *today* count. Even though you will still make mistakes, you can be thankful for God's special grace in forgiving your goof-ups.

We need to forgive ourselves for the past. You need to forgive yourself for all the things you've done. Until you ask for God's forgiveness and accept it as a free gift, you'll never be able to forgive yourself or understand what living a joy-filled life is all about.

And you need to forgive your mom and dad for getting a divorce. To forgive your older sister for not being able to be there for you when you needed someone. Your sister has yet to understand how God has changed your life. In time she'll see the example that you can be for Christ in your own home. Instead of thinking you need help, she'll want to know more about the difference God has made in your life. Sure, things won't always be easy. But God can give meaning and purpose to all you are and everything you do.

When I was a kid, I was running down the sidewalk one day after school and *splat!* I almost knocked down a grown man twice my size. As he grabbed me, I was glad to hear him laughing and to see that it was my minister, not some stranger who was going to be mad at me for not watching where I was going.

He also surprised me with these words, "When you're unhappy, it shows all over your face."

How did he know that I had a lot on my mind? I wondered. I asked him, "Do you think I have an unhappy face?"

"Yes, I do."

He was right. And it wasn't long before I was spilling out some of the things that were going on in my life. After we'd talked for a while, he asked, "Donalyn, what do you think God meant when He said He wanted us to have an *abundant* life?"

That very moment I could feel a smile creep across my face. Without hesitation I answered, "He wanted us to have the good things in life."

"And do you have that in your life right now?"

My answer had to be "no."

Later, when I was a little older, I first realized that I'm the only one responsible for *who* I am and what I'm *doing*. The realization hit me hard. I knew I had a lifetime of choices I had to make.

Heather, you've been through a great deal at a young age, and so many of the things you were involved in made you unhappy. When you accepted Jesus into your life— and all your so-called friends took off—it was only natural that you'd want to be with the Lord. You thought heaven would be so much better—and it will! But God has timed your life. Don't take away from Him the gifts you can give Him by living as a lighted candle in a dark world.

The Lord doesn't want you to take your life, Heather. His arms are reaching for you—to give you encouragement and a full, happy life.

At this moment, I am holding you next to my heart. When you get discouraged, remember how important you are to the Lord. As you grow with Him and learn to believe in yourself, the fear that you'll take your own life will fade and finally pass away. Instead, you'll be more concerned about not having enough hours in the day to do all the things you want to do.

The Lord has put you in a place where He can use you the most. The story you heard on the radio about the girl who was a prostitute and drug addict is an example of how important it is to talk about what the Lord has done for you. For your friends and family, your life may be the only example they'll ever see of the difference God can make in a person's life. Share God's love and continue to read His Word, so you'll know His truths and His answers for you.

What greater joy can there be than to meet the Lord knowing that you fulfilled His purpose for your life?

Where Are You Going?

Hey, Scarecrow. You look like you could use a workout."

"If you think I'm in rough shape, take a look at yourself. You don't look very happy. What's wrong?"

"Nothing ever turns out right for me. I can't seem to do anything right."

"You can do things you never thought you could do, if you *believe in yourself*. A long time ago, nations would choose a soldier to fight in their place. One nation chose a giant, but the other nation knew of no one who would face the giant. A young, inexperienced boy believed that he could beat the giant. He prayed, asking God to give him the courage he needed to fight the giant. With God's help, and believing in himself, he beat the giant. And his nation

won. . . .Hey, where are you
going?"
"I can't hang around here. I've
got things to do!"

7

A Mother's Prayer

Dear Lord,

It's me again—Mary. I know for the last two days it seems as though every breath I've taken has been in prayer to you. I'm so confused. I thought if I came and prayed in this chapel I would feel your presence closer to me. How I need you to fill me with your strength.

I'd give anything to wake from this nightmare and find out it was only a dream. Then all three of my children would be with me and Robert wouldn't be in this hospital, dying. Lord, what amount of suffering caused him to try and hang himself? Why didn't I *know* the pain he was going through? Why couldn't I have been there to stop him? Now I feel dead inside.

What was I to do? He was my son, and I didn't want him to suffer any more. The doctors told me he was brain dead, his lungs had collapsed and he was bleeding internally. Only the respirator was keeping him alive. How long could I let him live like that? My heart was breaking. What can I do?

But when I have to face his younger brother and sister—I don't know what I'll say to them. They're only children. They don't understand what's happened. *I* don't understand. How can I help them struggle through their pain, when I don't know how to bear my *own*?

Lord, you are my only hope. Pour your words into my

heart so I'll know what to say to them. Give me the strength I need to hold us together as a family.

The day Robert was born I thanked you for giving me a beautiful son. I can still feel the joy I felt the first time I held "my Bobby" in my arms. Now I've given him back to you. He's been a good boy, and I know you love him. All my children are in your hands.

So am I.

Robert committed suicide July 31, 1985. He was taken off the respirator August 2, at 8:15 a.m. and died at 10:30 a.m. the same day.

Bobby's Memory

When he was only nine years old, I pretended not to see him place the card on his swing. I remember the tears that fell as I read his words, "Mom, thanks for loving me."

As He was growing up, if he could only have remembered to replace the pain with the *love*, he would have chosen to live. He would be with me today.

8

In the Middle

Dear Donalyn,

My brother Keith was a troubled child ever since I can remember. When he was little, he threw terrible, long temper tantrums. Nobody could get near him. These continued until he was nine or ten and finally subsided. But his internal anguish took on other forms. Sometimes he would refuse to go to school. He would even threaten to kill himself at the dinner table with the steak knives.

When Keith was 17, he moved into a boarding house. He worked at a veterinary clinic and planned to go to college and med school when he finished high school. Four months before graduation, he was taken into police custody when he unknowingly accompanied a friend on a burglary. When the police phoned my mom to tell her, she blew up and refused to go see him. The minute she hung up I knew she wanted to kick herself.

But I couldn't turn my back on him.

I drove an hour into town and took Keith to a coffee shop to talk. I insisted he go and talk to Mom. That was a big mistake. I treated him as if he had no other choice than to go see her. In his mind, she'd caused him a lifetime of problems.

Three long hours we sat at Mom's house, listening to her apologize for everything from pinning his diapers wrong to having divorced Keith's dad, to not knowing his real needs. She was in tears, pleading for another chance. Keith sat across the room with his back turned, stone cold and silent.

I got frustrated. I tried to "muscle him." "You don't have to forgive her or *love* her," I said, "but you *will*, this weekend, move back home and live under this roof until you finish high school. Then you won't have to support yourself. You can save money and move out the day you graduate."

That was on a Wednesday night. I drove him back to jail at midnight. On Saturday afternoon, the day before he was due to move back home—at least according to my "divine plan"—Mom had *another* change of heart.

"If Keith is that miserable with me, I'll not only let him live away from home, I'll *pay* his rent. Please call and tell him that for me."

Keith never got the phone call. At 7 P.M. I tried to call Mom. Keith was dead. His body had been found in an alley by a local department store. I became frantic when Mom didn't answer her phone or door. I was so afraid that Keith had murdered Mom, then killed himself. He hated her that much.

When I found Mom, she was okay—at least physically. But Keith's death had left her with more hurt than he'll ever know. We found out he had jumped off a parking garage at Wards, directly across the street from the hospital where he'd been born. His birth certificate was in his pocket. He had circled the blank spot where his father's name should have gone. (Mom's marriage to Keith's dad was annulled before his birth.) A search of his pockets also revealed a suicide note: "I have no father. I am a bastard."

That piece of paper is all Mom and I have left of Keith—except our guilt.

Love,
Kelly

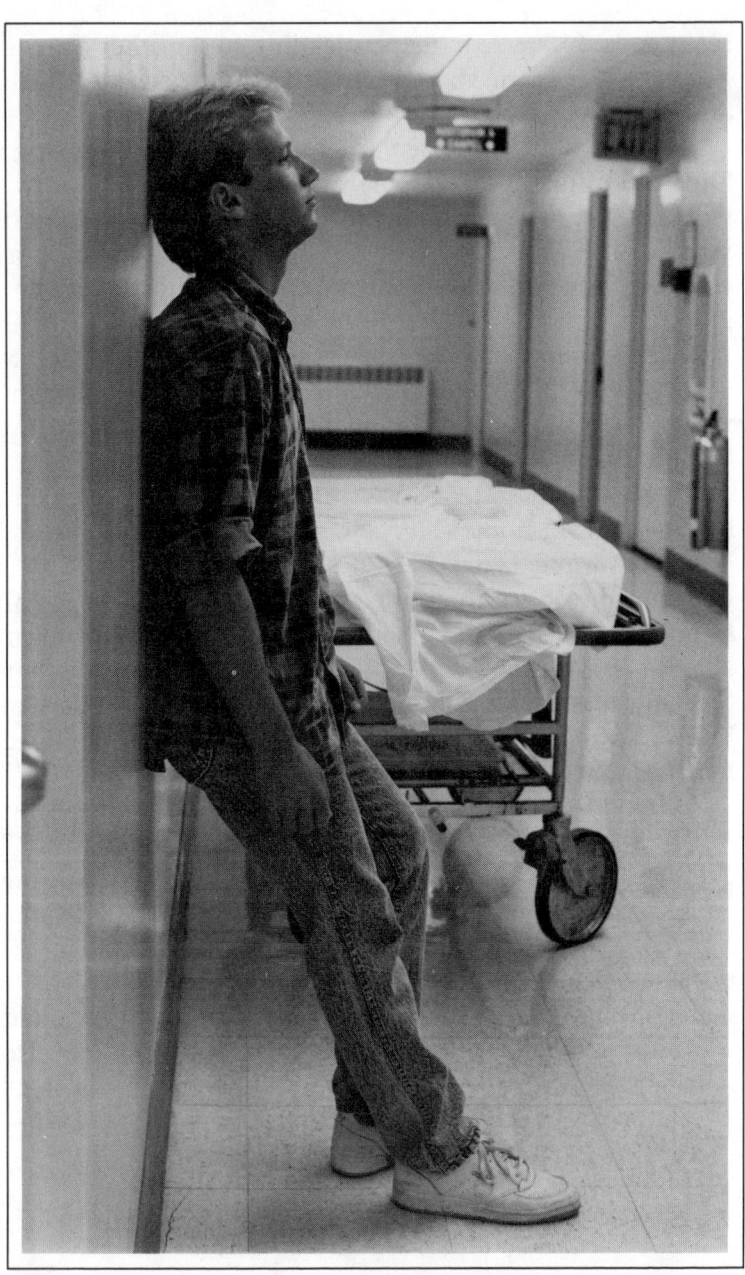

Suicide

He's Dead
He's Dead
He's Dead
He's Dead
He's Dead
He's Dead
He's Dead

Dear Kelly,

It isn't easy being in the middle, is it? Or to find ways to mend relationships—especially in a family. It's a heavy burden for anyone to carry, especially when it involves people you love. And when your brother took his own life, nothing was settled. You feel you'll always remain in the middle.

How do you move forward when everything has stopped? That's a hard question. But you can begin by trying to understand.

Your mother's anger and her refusal to see your brother was her first reaction to the shocking news that he was in trouble with the police. I think you know that she wouldn't have let him stay in jail. But you saw yourself as the only one who could help him. It never seems to work when we think we're responsible for someone else's life. Making excuses for the behavior of others never changes anything, nor does it help them.

We can *be there* for them—willing to love and understand them—but they have to take the responsibility for their own life, or they'll never learn to take care of themselves.

It seems obvious to me that your brother had a mind of his own. You shouldn't feel guilty because you encouraged him to go home and talk with your mother. You had no way of knowing, and perhaps he didn't either, what the outcome would be.

Because Keith was unable to handle his own feelings, it seems to me he was very good at letting everyone else feel guilty. Your mother spent hours apologizing for almost everything she had done "wrong" in her life. Maybe this continued to encourage Keith to feel that everything wrong in his life was her fault. Sitting across the room, stone cold and with his back turned to your mother was his way of saying, "You hurt me, so I'll hurt you."

What I'm saying may seem very cold, but it's not meant to be that way. Keith had lost control of his feelings and his behavior. He didn't know how to put together the pieces of his own life and he was hurting so much that he lashed out in pain. His reactions hurt not only him but everyone around him. If he had a choice, he wouldn't have wanted things to be this way.

At an early age your brother began to show signs of not being able to handle his emotions. Not knowing how to properly express his feelings, he allowed his emotions to run wild. Many people have to deal with a problem just like your brother's every day. Through professional help they begin recognizing their behavior patterns. They learn to calm down the moment they begin to feel uncontrollable outbursts of emotion.

When we're able to look at a situation calmly, we can better understand and accept the situation. Then we can make the correct decision and behave accordingly. In time, you're able to change an unacceptable learned behavior with a proper response to your emotions. No longer do these outbursts control your behavior. Once you've learned to control your behavior, you're able to have better relationships with others and live a full and productive life.

I can understand your working so hard to try and make things better in your home; and even though things didn't work out the way you would have wanted them to, you have no reason to feel guilty. How would you have felt if you had done nothing at all?

Guilt makes you feel so helpless. You want to turn back the clock. You want to do things differently. The "if only's" can go on forever. Guilt is just another burden, and God's Word tells us to bring our burdens to Him. When we feel guilty for whatever reason, we should remember to give our feelings to the Lord and ask Him to help us forgive ourselves and heal our broken heart. Focusing attention on the past, we'll never be able to give today and tomorrow all that we have.

Keith's decision to take his own life was his. The note he left was a cry of pain. Keith wasn't a "bastard," he was a young man who was hurting and he didn't know how else to express his pain. I'm thankful that our heavenly father understands pain. God comforts the broken-hearted, and His understanding goes beyond our own. God also knows the pain you and your mother are feeling. He has always been there waiting for you. Give Him your guilt and allow Him to help bear your anguish.

I cannot begin to explain why there is suffering in our world. It's a fact of life that no one is free from living through disappointments or experiencing great pain. I thank God that we do not have to experience this alone. I think the greatest pain of all would be not having Christ in our lives to share our burdens. What a blessing it is to know that there's not one thing in our lives that we have to carry alone.

We can let suffering end our lives or hold us back from living our life at its full potential. Because the love of the Lord is freely given, the choice is ours to make: to move toward death, or life.

I've seen God use tragedy in the lives of others to prepare them for a greater ministry. And because of the pain they experienced, they were able to understand and help someone else that was hurting.

Suffering can also give us a closer relationship with God as we learn to share everything with Him.

Kelly, I am certain that you have a deeper understanding for those who are hurting. You may have just the right words inside of you that will help someone else think twice before trying to take their own life. Let the Lord guide you in His direction and His purpose.

When you have a willing heart, God can use you to reach out to others when no one else can understand.

I know if you ask Him to take this tragedy and turn it around for Him, He will. Wait and see.

Under Wraps

It's Christmas morning, and I just know I'm getting a model plane. It's the only present I've asked for all year. I told them the model I wanted, what store it was in and how much it cost. There isn't any way they could have forgotten.

Where's my model plane? There were so many beautiful presents under the tree, how could one of them *not* be what I really wanted?

Then I heard a voice. "Here's another present with your name on it. Do you want to know what it is?"

"Father, does it matter what it is? I didn't get the one present I asked for."

"Don't let your disappointment keep you from opening a present that could hold something better that you ever dreamed of."

9

The Promise

Jake, wake up! It's me—Chris.

Chris, what are you doing here?

I came to help you.

Help me? With what?

Jake, don't play games with me. I know what's going on. I came back to stop you from committing suicide.

Why do you want to do that? *You* did it!

I didn't know what I was doing.

That's hard to believe. You planned every detail—from the letters you left to the gun you used to kill yourself.

Jake, listen—I'm trying to tell you I didn't know what I was doing! I was only 17. I had my whole life in front of me. I made a mistake—a tragic mistake. And now I'm trying to keep you from making the same one.

Chris, why *did* you kill yourself? You had everything going for you. You were the top player on our school hockey team. Everyone liked you. Good grades were a breeze for you. I wish they were as easy for me. Everything you did you always did well.

You know why, Jake? Because I tried to control every situation in my life. I had to do my best at everything, and I expected too much from others. When things didn't work out according to my perfect plan, it was hard for me to handle. I got so caught up with losing the first girl I thought I loved that I couldn't see any further than my own feelings of hurt and rejection. If I had only stopped

92

to think about what I was doing, I would have realized that just because one relationship doesn't work out it doesn't mean you'll never have another one.

And you know what else? I didn't think about my family, or what it would do to my parents. I really didn't think about being dead—about the finality of it. I didn't have the perfect plan. Neither do you.

Jake, I can't stop you from killing yourself, but I beg you to think about what it would mean. I know how you feel deep down in your gut. I couldn't see anything in myself worth living for, either. But you must make yourself see your life further than where you are right now. Give yourself a chance to get through your feelings of hurt and helplessness.

There is a perfect plan, a plan that brings hope and life and joy back again. But it's not in us. You don't have to carry your feelings all by yourself. Other people care and God cares. I know that now. God sees so much more in us than we see in ourselves. I know that sounds really simple, but it's true. It's only when we climb out of our own problems and reach out to God and others around us that we receive the love and understanding that we all need.

Jake, it's time for me to go. Look—the rain has stopped. And there's a rainbow through the trees! Think about it. The rainbow reminds us of the promise from God that He will carry us through every mistake, every disappointment, every tear—and He'll wipe them away with His love.

———

"Jake, wake up!"

"Mom?"

"I've been calling for you for the last ten minutes. Are you all right? You look pale."

"Yeah . . . Hey Mom! Come over to my window and look at this rainbow. Isn't it great?"

"It's beautiful. Wish we could look at it all day, but there's a lot we have to do. I've got to get ready—and so do you. Breakfast in five minutes!"

———————

"Hey, Chris—it's more than beautiful. It's a promise. I'm going to live."

Friends First

It took a broken relationship and time to teach me that a shattered heart does mend. It's not the end of the world if I don't have a date on Saturday night, or if I never exchange class rings. Real love begins with *friendship*, and it's important to take it one day at a time.

On the Occasion of Chris's Memorial Service

I have just a few words to say to the people in this congregation. My fond hope is that they will somehow have an impact—on you and all those you touch.

You see before you a grieving parent who has suffered an irreplaceable loss. As I look around this room and remember what happened at our home, I feel all of your help, love and support. Yet, in spite of it all, I am still struck by one thought. All this outpouring of love, all these generous gifts of time, affection and genuine caring are so much appreciated—but none of it can bring back our Chris. We have to come to grips with the fact that he is gone from this earth. Forever.

And so I have a message I would like to leave with you young people. I pray it will influence any of you who suffer from the same trouble and torment that Chris did that led him to take his own life.

It's this: If you or a friend are going through something that makes you feel desperate, that makes you consider doing what Chris did, then I ask you . . . I urge you . . . no, I *plead* with you to reach out to someone before you commit that final act.

Reach out to a friend. He will listen, understand, and help. Reach out to your family, in spite of what you think they will say. You'll find love and understanding from them, and some way of handling your problem. And if all that fails, then for God's sake, reach out to a minister, a priest, a rabbi, a counselor. There are thousands of them all over the United States who are ready, willing and anxious to share God's love and a better sense of purpose than taking your own life.

I beg you—reach out!

Chris's Dad

Excerpted from a message delivered on
October 27, 1984 at Dunwoody Methodist Church
in Atlanta, Georgia.

10

Buried Secrets

Dear Donalyn,

I was the one who found him. I thought maybe something was wrong when we were together the night before. Todd looked at me so funny when he kissed me. Then he said goodbye and drove away. I tried to call him all night long. I couldn't understand where he could be.

He had an apartment within walking distance from my dorm room on campus. I was so scared. He didn't tell me he was going anywhere. Why didn't he answer the phone? The next morning really early, I ran over to his apartment and banged on the door. No one answered. When I reached for the door I found it unlocked, so I walked in.

His bedroom door was shut. I knocked and yelled, "Todd, open the door!" But he didn't answer. I was really getting scared. I yelled again and shoved the door open.

And there he was. I'll never forget it. All that blood on those white sheets and on the floor. I wanted to scream, but I couldn't talk—it was like my voice and my legs and everything were frozen. I thought I should call the hospital, but I couldn't move.

Just then, Todd's brother walked in and saw the whole mess. He made me go sit in the living room. All I could hear were a bunch of fuzzy words that drifted in and out. Two other guys rushed in to help his brother carry Todd out.

But as they were carrying him, Todd groaned and I'll never forget thinking, "He's alive!" Todd didn't want to go anywhere. He kicked one of the guys when they were putting him in the back seat of the car.

I couldn't believe how strong he was, even after losing all that blood!

Someone else picked me up and took me to the hospital. I don't remember who. It was like being in a dream in slow motion.

When I got to the hospital, Todd's mom and dad were there. She screamed at me—that it was all my fault. Over and over: "What did you *do* to him?"

So I ran—away from the hospital, with all the ugly sights and sounds and smells and all the people's faces staring at me.

In the hospital, they put him in the psych ward, with people who act really crazy. I didn't see him or hear from him. After he'd been in the hospital for two months, they told me he was going home. I knew no one had cleaned up his room since the day he left. So I did. It took hours, but I cleaned up all the dried blood. I didn't want him to have to come back to that mess. It made me sick—actually sick—and I cried for a while.

Then I opened his closet. Any other time Todd was a slob. But everything was neatly placed in bags—with people's names on them. All his clothes were washed and hung up. There was even a bag for me with a cassette tape in it, but I was too scared to play that tape to hear what he had to say.

That was when it hit me. Todd had *really wanted* to kill himself! How come I didn't know? Was I weird, or something, to have a boyfriend like that? I must be a real nerd.

That's when I decided not to tell anyone about what happened. If I told anyone, they'd think Todd and I were both freaks. It was no problem keeping this a secret. Todd's parents covered it up, too. No one in school knew. They thought Todd had gotten real sick and had to stay home for a while.

But I can't cover up what's going on inside *me*. What's wrong with me? I keep crying. Inside, I keep wondering if it *is* my fault. What did I do that made him cut himself all over like that? How come I end up with the weird boyfriends?

Todd tried to kill himself a year ago today. I still feel like my stomach's being torn apart. But I'm scared to tell anybody—even you—because I'm afraid you'll think I'm stupid or weird.

Carmen

Why?

Why is it that some people
fight to stay alive
and others choose to die
by their own hand?

Dear Carmen,

Being able to share what you've held inside for so long was the beginning of your healing. You will never *forget* those experiences, but you *can* get over them and go on with your life.

When you go through a traumatic experience, it's normal to feel as though you're going through it in a daze. Your reactions are slower because you're in a state of shock. I think it's our mind's way of getting us through that experience so we don't fall apart.

When you reached the hospital and Todd's mother screamed at you, it was just her way of denying that her son did not want to go on living. She blamed you needlessly. The shock and hurt she felt kept her from stopping long enough to try and understand what had happened, or to take the time to talk with you. She was desperately trying to find someone to blame because of the deep pain she felt.

If you think back to the times in your own life when you've gotten upset, I'll bet you can recall saying things you really didn't mean. As we all do, I'll bet you've also directed your guilt or pain at someone else by blaming them. The person who says hurting words may get over it and not even remember what he said. But the person who *heard* them may continue to be upset for a long time. Hurting words, taken to your heart, can cause you to question yourself and feel insecure about your behavior.

We all need to remember that what we say can become a powerful weapon to hurt or to build. Offer words of understanding when others are going through a difficult time and we bring people together. We need to lean on each other. It's so important that we ask the Lord to give us the right kind of hearts and the words to say when someone is hurting. The first step in working out problems is *always* going to God in prayer. God also has an answer for those of us that have *been* hurt by the actions of others. By asking Him to forgive those who have hurt us, He heals our hearts. The memory will always be there, but the pain won't be the same.

Time also heals our wounds, and it allows us some distance to look at what really happened. It gives us a chance to try to understand. You know what *really* happened. Don't look for something you didn't do, just because someone shot blame in your direction. Don't let those words strip you of all your worth.

You're so close to the situation, Carmen—and you're feeling so badly about yourself—you can't see all the good others see in you right now. What a caring heart you have! You didn't just think about yourself. You went back to Todd's room. (I think it was also your way of trying to understand what had happened.)

And no, you're not weird. Todd isn't weird either. Todd was having a hard time coping with his own feelings. That doesn't mean, however, that in time he can't go on to live a full and happy life. Todd wasn't being honest about his feelings with himself or others around him. I bet if you asked Todd today he would tell you it wasn't the right thing to do.

When we feel like giving up it's hard to remember that these depressed feelings won't last forever. It's like having a huge pile of papers stacked on your desk. Then one day you're looking for some papers you think you've lost. It isn't until you go through the papers stacked on your desk that you find what you were looking for. Our feelings can be just like that stack of papers. Sometimes sad feelings are stacked on top of the good feelings, and we have to really look in order to find the feelings of wanting to live. Even though it's been there all along.

There was no way you could have known Todd was going to try and kill himself unless he shared those feelings with you. When someone we're close to is going through a hard time, we may be aware that something's wrong, but we can't know what they're *thinking* unless they tell us.

I'm sorry that his parents wanted to hide what happened to him, because it made you feel like you had to hide *your* feelings. I'm so thankful we don't have to hide our feelings from God. We can come to Him with all our feelings, even when the words are too hard to say.

At some point
everyone
needs
someone
to
lean
on.

11

"Dear Father . . ."

Dear Donalyn,

For sixteen years I thought my dad was dead. Mom had made up a pretty good story, and I believed her. There was no reason for me not to believe her. No one in the family ever talked about Dad, so I never questioned what she told me. And whenever I tried to ask Mom about my father she would start to cry. I didn't want to hurt her, so I kept most of my questions to myself.

Then, about six months ago, someone told me my father wasn't dead. So I confronted Mom. She said, "He wasn't ready to be a father." She said she was going to tell me the truth someday, but she didn't want to "hurt" me.

I got so upset that I spent the rest of the night alone in my room. Mom came and knocked on my door, but I didn't want to talk to her.

I spent the next several days trying to get things straight in my own head. So many of the things I did were secretly for my father. I'd always wanted him to be proud of me— if he were alive. I guess I'd put together this fantasy picture of my dad.

But the person I had made up in my own mind didn't exist. It was like someone had died all over again. But, he was never dead. There was no perfect hero. Just this man who'd taken off because he couldn't handle being my father. Why didn't he care? What did I ever do to him?

112

I kept thinking about Mom and what she could have done with her life if I'd never been born. Maybe my parents would have stayed together. I knew Mom still loved him. I wanted to die.

I began to plan how I would commit suicide.

Two days before I was going to kill myself, I wanted to make things up with Mom. I came home from school and told her I was sorry about getting so upset. She understood. She said she would have been upset if she were me. I told her I knew she'd given up a lot for me—and if I were dead she could live the rest of her life the way she wanted to. She asked if I'd thought about committing suicide and I said, "Wouldn't that solve everyone's problems?"

Mom started crying. And then she grabbed me and asked me if I thought killing myself would change anything for me. She told me it would change *everything* for her. Her life would become a nightmare.

I learned a lot that night. I realized how much my mom loves me. She *wasn't* still in love with my father. And she didn't feel like she ever wanted to get married again. Mom told me that I keep her going, and she would rather have God take *her* life than to live without me. She said every day of my life I was helping her fulfill her dream of being a mother.

Then she reminded me of something she's said many times: "I will not always be right in how I try to teach you, but I always want to protect you from a lot of hurt."

Mom gave me a big hug. Both of us were sorry for everything that had happened. She told me my father really left because he was selfish—he didn't want to think about anyone other than himself. She didn't believe he really left because of me. He was just looking for an excuse, and if it wasn't me, in time he would have come up with another reason.

Things are going okay for me now that I know the truth. Mom and I are a lot closer. There are times when I really miss not having a father. I'll go over to a friend's house and his father will be there, and I can't help but wish I had a father.

But the man that left sixteen years ago was never a real father to me. Sometimes I wish I had a father to take his place. But it's okay.

David

In the Garden, One Flower

I had a dream last night
that I was standing in front of a
    wooden gate.
The gate was old and worn,
as if it had been used for many
    years,
and it appeared to open the way
    to a garden.
I couldn't make up my mind
if I wanted to go inside.
Then I heard someone say,
"Within this gate are flowers
    and trees,
alive with beauty greater
than anything you've ever
    seen."
Slowly I walked through the
    gate.
I couldn't believe my eyes!
I had never seen anything
    before
so perfect!
Except
my heart sank

when I looked down.
At my feet stood one flower,
plain and almost colorless,
large—too large—and wild
    grown,
out of place in this garden.
"How could this be? What went
    wrong?"
"This single flower will always
    grow in our garden,"
the voice said.
It's the most precious of all the
    other flowers,
a reminder that nothing is
    perfect
but
God's love for you.

Dear David,

Your hurt required compassion and understanding toward your mom. I think she would agree that telling you the truth from the start would have avoided a lot of problems. But because of her love for you she *thought* she was protecting you from your father's rejection.

It was a shock for you to find out the truth. But, in fact, you've been grieving for the "perfect" father that you had made up in your mind. And you didn't want to replace him with the father your mother told you about. The truth *does* hurt sometimes, but, given a choice I believe we'd all rather know the truth.

David, the problem was not you. It was with your father. I cannot answer for him, but he must have had some problems within himself that he couldn't handle. Maybe that's what made him react as if he didn't care. Nothing you did made him leave. You were only a small child. Your mother was most likely right when she told you he was just looking for an excuse. That doesn't make it right. But so often, people blame someone else for their feelings.

The conversation you had with your mother is a good example. More people should do what you did. When we face our problems and talk things out with a person we can trust and respect, we begin to find the answers we are searching for. We can also work out the conflicts we create in our minds. Sometimes we create worse problems for ourselves because we *think* we have an accurate picture— when really we *don't*. Just think, before you talked with your mom you were going to end your life! Now you see things differently.

And I'd guess your mom sees some things differently, too. So often, single parents feel they have the full responsibility of loving and protecting their child. They want to make up for the parent who's missing. My own mother wanted everything to be so perfect for me, trying to "compensate" for my illness. Our moms and dads sometimes like to think they can wrap a shield around us to protect us from anything that hurts. But they can't. No one can protect us from hurts or disappointments.

Whenever I had to face a problem, I knew my mom was there. But really it's the Lord who helps me make it through the hard times in my life. I think we forget how easy it is just to turn a problem over to God. How do you do this? By praying and asking the Lord to help you trust Him as He works things out according to His will.

I can understand how you feel as you watch your friends with their fathers. At 15, my heart ached. As I stood in front of my father, refusing to shed another tear, I said, "Daddy, just because you've left Mom doesn't mean you have to leave us kids." He never answered me. But he no longer remembered birthdays or Christmas presents or shared my dreams of going to college.

In the space of one afternoon, I no longer had a father. Nothing after that would have been as important to me as getting a hug and knowing that he loved me. I wished my father could have said just a few words that would have helped me understand. I wouldn't have felt so rejected and unworthy of being loved. I asked myself, "What's wrong with me that Daddy doesn't care?" At my friends' homes, I saw a mom and dad and kids—all together—just the way my family *should* have been. But I wasn't as upset about my parents getting a divorce as I was about not having a father, someone to go to when I had a problem.

Later, I discovered that my father didn't know how to tell us he was going through some personal problems. Although I tried to understand, it didn't make up for his absence. I know my family could have gotten through this much easier if we had continued to communicate more openly with one another.

Then one day I prayed, "Dear Father," instead of "Dear Jesus." At that very moment I stopped praying. I hesitantly said those precious words again, "Dear Father." An empty gap filled in my heart, and I began to cry. For the first time in my life I realized I *had* a father. A Wonderful Father! In His faithfulness, He had always been there for me—protecting me, loving me and healing my wounds.

So often we search for answers in empty places, when our heavenly Father can help us understand situations we cannot change. It was the love of my true Father that taught me *I am someone* and *I am worthy of being loved*. He also changed my hurting heart to a forgiving heart.

David, you also have a Father. Those of us who have longed for a parent can know we have a perfect heavenly Father who is watching us grow, a Father who will continue to be at our side while He molds us to carry out His plan for our lives.

There are so many things my heavenly Father has taught me—but the most important lesson I've learned was remembering that He is *my Father* and I am *His child*.

Did I tell you about a man
    named Jesus?
He fed multitudes.
The winds and the water obeyed
    Him.
He was strong, yet humble.
In His wisdom, He knew
how to answer every man.
In His heart,
there is a place
for every one of His children—
where burdens are lighter
and every joy is greater.
We are the children
He holds in the palm of His
    hand.

12

A Hiding Place

"Grandpa, how long has this window been open in the old barn?"

"Oh, for a long time. I took down part of the wood I nailed up just in case anyone decided to use it for a hiding place."

"What do you mean, a hiding place?"

"You were too little to remember, but once when your older brother was growing up, he was looking for a hiding place. One night he wanted to get out of doing his chores so he could leave early for a basketball game at school. He'd already put his chores off for several days, so your mom wasn't going to let him go until he'd done his work.

"Well, he got mad and felt no one cared about what *he* wanted to do. He made up his mind he'd hide out in the old barn until morning came so he could run away. When everyone thought he was out doing his chores, he took off for the barn. He noticed a storm was coming up, so he slammed the front door tight. Inside, it was completely dark and he couldn't see anything at all. He tried to get out, but the old rusty latch had locked from the outside.

"About that time, he was getting scared. He could hear the lightning and thunder from outside. Being stuck in the old barn wasn't part of his plan. He yelled for the family, but there was not any way we could have heard him. When your mom couldn't find your brother, she thought he had gone to the game without telling her. Meanwhile, your brother was cold and scared, but he found his way to a corner in the barn where he had a chance to think about what he'd done.

"He began to realize that if he had done his chores, none of this would have happened. And he could have gone to the game with his friends. He wasn't sure when he would get out of that old barn. And he didn't treasure the idea of spending the night there with a storm coming up. He began to remember the fun times he used to have with his family, and he even remembered the times your mom asked him what he wanted to do. He realized that his mom *did* care about him. He was feeling bad about running away, because he would have been leaving everyone who cared about him. He was so tired he fell asleep.

"When it got late, your mom was worried. After calling his friends, she called me. The storm hadn't let up, but she insisted we go out and look for him. After, we sat up all night and I watched her walk the floor. I knew if something happened to your brother, she'd blame herself.

"At first light, the storm had passed. She grabbed her coat and began to walk across the farm. I thought I'd better follow her in case she needed me. About that time, your brother woke up. He tried again to get out, but he couldn't. He began to yell for your mom. I couldn't hear him, but she could. I watched her run toward the barn as fast as she could. Once she opened the door, he flew into her arms. By the time I got there, I wanted to tan his hide— but your mom wouldn't hear of it.

"That night I overheard your mom and brother when they said good night.

" 'I'm really sorry, Mom.

" 'I was so afraid because I thought I'd lost you!' "

Maybe

Maybe we ought to hug others
a little more often
and tell them, "I love you."

13

A Reason to Live

My arms held her as she repeated the words over and over again—"I'm so tired of hurting." As I wiped the tears from her face, I gently spoke these words, "Do you know there isn't a tear that falls that God doesn't hear or see?" I saw her eyes look to me as if her heart were asking if these words were really true.

Her bedroom door opened a crack. I watched her four-year-old brother open the door just wide enough to come in. With all the concern in the world on his little face, he stood hesitant by the door. I stretched out my arms, giving him permission to come closer. As I hugged him, both he and his sister turned their eyes toward mine. I smiled and asked, "Would you like me to tell you a story?" In the pause that followed, I saw the light shining through the bedroom window and remembered Christ's words: *I am the light of the world.*

Silently I prayed, *Father, fill my heart with your words.* Their young faces watched my every move, waiting for me to begin. And this is the story I told:

Once upon a time there was a boy and girl who lived in two different parts of the world. They were thoughtful and kind to everyone they met. Though they had a lot of friends, neither one could see himself as others did. They were always giving their love away, but never thought of the love that others had for them. In their minds, they were

131

never good enough or attractive enough, and they felt their dreams would never come true. When they were happy, they brightened everyone's days; but they also had times when they would cry when no one was around.

Even though they lived very far apart and had never met each other, they began to share the same feelings. They decided they didn't want to live anymore, so they chose to take their own lives in their hands and commit suicide.

That afternoon, the girl's mother had gone shopping after work and saw a lovely sweater she thought would look beautiful on her daughter. She drove home, looking forward to surprising her daughter with a gift. As she walked into her daughter's room, she pressed the sweater tightly against her heart. There was silence for a moment. Then a long pause separated each word as the mother cried, "I love you, and I bought this sweater for you!" She laid the sweater across her daughter and rocked her cold, dead body in her arms.

Meanwhile, the boy's little brother had run through the front door calling out his older brother's name. As the little boy walked down the hall, he saw that his brother's bedroom door was open, so he went in to say hello. There on the floor, in a pool of blood, lay his brother's body. Trembling in shock, the little boy turned and ran out of the house into the rain.

Only moments passed before his parents came home. The rain and the tears now covered their small son's face. He spoke and the parents ran to their older son. As the father lifted his older son in his arms the little boy cried, "We can't play anymore."

Now together, the boy and girl stood at an open gate. Searching for a voice they could not find, they turned around—then around again. But the voice continued echoing, "If they could see our faces, feel our pain that will never heal . . ." No other words were spoken as their feelings of uncertainty grew stronger.

Finally the silence was broken. "What should we do?" asked the girl. Before the boy could answer her they were silenced by another voice. "It was not God's time for you to be with Him. You chose the time. Look back on what your actions have done and all that you've missed. Both of you had lost your trust in God for your future. You also forgot to pray. Even though God already know's our hurts and disappointments, you still needed to tell Him in prayer; that is the beginning of your willingness to receive God's direction and not your own.

"It was God's desire for you both to fulfill His will for your lives, to discover that He wanted to be with you always. If you had only looked beyond the pain and trusted in Him, He could have shown you how much there was to live for. The love He has for us would have carried you through this time in your lives. Jesus did not come just to be our Savior, but He also came to be our life."

The story told and with a heart that was filled with the reminder of God's unfailing love for us, I asked the girl in my arms, "Do you know how precious you are to God?"

With tears of hope she cried, "Now I know I have a reason to live."

Daniel was a white and graceful
   seagull.
He had everything to live for.
But things didn't go right.
He gave up.
He didn't want to live anymore.
The other seagulls thought,
"If Daniel gave up, we should
   give up, too."
One seagull thought for a very
   long time, though.
While the others folded up their
   wings
miserably,
he kept his eyes open wide and
   his wings free to fly.
And he was the only one who
   felt
when the new wind of morning
brought freshness and
lift.

14

The Colors of Your Heart

As I walked past the chapel today, I stopped to look at the light as it bounced colors off the stained glass window. The colors were beautiful as they fell so gently. I ran to look at all the other windows, but only one reflected the light. Then I thought, "The colors must be inside."

A silent prayer ran through my head: "Please, Lord. Have the door open so I can get in."

My excitement grew as I reached for the knob—and the door quietly opened. The moment I stepped inside, my excitement slowed and changed into reverence. Colors graced the aisle that led me to the altar. At the foot of the altar lay a color, shaped like a heart. I was aware of His holy presence. Raising my eyes toward the cross, I knelt.

"Lord, what are the colors of my heart? How broken has my path been to your altar? If my heart loses its radiance, show me *your* light. Always lead me on the path that comes to your altar." I lifted my hands to wipe my tears, for I'd felt His love despite my unworthiness. I stood and walked down the aisle, realizing my love for the Lord would reflect the colors of my heart. If I trust in Him, He *will* direct all the paths of my life.

When I reached the door, I turned to look at the altar one last time. It reminded me about the altar inside each one of us, the silent space where God meets us—where He accepts us and the prayer we offer to Him.

Then I swung the door open wide and ran down the steps. My heart was filled with joy! I was taking the Lord with me.

15

A Letter Just for You

Our walk is over, but I will always have a special place in my heart for you. We've been through a lot together—you and I—tears and laughter, sorrow and hope. If I could only go around the world and share precious moments with each and every one of you! I can't, of course, but God can.

I want you to remember: No matter how unworthy you may feel, or how often you think you've failed to measure up, hold the truths of Christ close to your heart.

You are special to God. Because of His love for us, He sent His only Son so that we would have eternal life through Christ. He created you in His image, and you are the only one that can carry out His plans for your life.

What does God want from us? He wants us to love Him. When you can't find a reason to go on, *just love Him.* When you feel you've disappointed God and everyone around, *just love Him.*

As you love the Lord, He'll give you a reason to live. When you think you've failed, you'll find His forgiveness. And when you think you can't go on, you'll find His strength. There is no burden God cannot carry, no pain He cannot bear.

There's a special letter I've been saving till now to share with you. I met the young woman who wrote it in Chicago when I'd gone there to speak at a teen retreat. She was seventeen, so alive and beautiful. Raised in a Christian home, she'd attended a Christian high school. Until this weekend she was unable to share her problems with anyone. Now she realized that reaching out when she needed help was the first step to finding the answers she desperately needed.

I shared her tears—and how well I knew her pain! We took a long walk together, and that night the Lord helped her share some of her deepest hurts and disappointments. And in God's way, as we talked and prayed, He opened up thoughts and answers with possibilities. I want to share with you a small part of her letter that is so special for me:

> . . . *About life at home—you were right! Things are so much better. We still have our bad days, but they're fewer and further between. And they're made easier because I know my heavenly Father is looking down on me, longing to hold me in His arms and make everything right.*
>
> *One night, when I was crying, I thought about how much it must have hurt God when He created me to know that I'd have to hurt this much. He wouldn't have let it happen to me if there wasn't a purpose. So I think He must have something wonderful planned for me to do. I only wish the process weren't so painful!*
>
> *"The Lord will fulfill his purpose for me; your love, O Lord, endures forever—do not abandon the works of your hands" (Psalm 138:8, NIV).*

She had chosen the words of David. In David's greatest time of need, he praised the Lord and cried out to Him in faith—knowing that God would not abandon him and that He would carry out His purpose for David's life. She'd learned that loving God doesn't give us a life without hurts or disappointments. But God can help us make it through those times and things do get better.

When we look to God for His answers, we have a reason to live as we wait for His purpose to be revealed in our lives. In every burden I've ever known I have found a

141

blessing and a purpose. It wasn't always at the time I thought it would be—but it always came when I was ready to receive it.

Never give up! When God takes something away, He gives us something else in return. Live with the confidence that God holds all your tomorrows. Fill your mind with His purpose for your life and then you'll know His reason to live. Keep your eyes open wide, your hands free to help a friend, your heart filled with all the good things God intended for you. And always, *always believe in yourself and in your dreams.*

Be joyful in hope, patient in affliction, faithful in prayer (Romans 12:12, NIV).

God Bless You,
Donalyn

He shall be as the light of the
    morning;
A cloudless sunrise
When the tender grass
Springs forth upon the earth;
As sunshine after rain.
And it is my family
He has chosen!
Yes, God has made
An everlasting covenant with
    me;
His agreement is eternal, final,
    sealed.
He will constantly look after
My safety and success.

2 Samuel 23:4–5, TLB

16

A Final Word:
The Facts About Suicide

5:30 A.M. The Emergency Room was as noisy as ever. A patient was rushed in on a rescue squad stretcher, with the crew pumping on his chest and bagging oxygen into his lungs. I hurried into the cardiac room behind the ER doctor and noted the patient with surprise and anguish. He could not have been more then 16 or 17 years old!

Numbly pitching-in with the vigorous efforts (though we knew them already to be futile), all of the doctors, nurses and technicians avoided the pain in each other's eyes. The rope burns on his neck told the story: he had hung himself.

Still I kept feeling for a pulse that would not come. I wanted desperately to make him live, to bring him back to life. *To give anew the gift of life—that's what we are here for*, I kept thinking. But we could not reverse the lack of oxygen to his brain. We could not give him thoughts or hopes or dreams again. He had extinguished them all, by his own hand, in a moment of pain—with a piece of rope.

I looked at the family, huddling together hopelessly, and I will never forget their shocked faces, the depth of their pain. Nor will I forget the police, standing awkwardly in the background, who had to question the parents because of his violent death.

Suicide now ranks as the second leading cause of death among 15- to 19-year-olds in the United States, representing a 41 percent increase over the last decade.[1] Even these startling statistics are probably far below the actual number, because suicides and suicidal attempts are vastly under-reported.

Between 50 to 75 percent of the adolescents who attempt suicide suffer from depression. Teens with conduct disorders are the second largest group of those who commit or attempt suicide, and those suffering from psychotic disorders such as schizophrenia represent the third largest group.[2] Teens considered at higher risk for suicide include those involved in substance abuse, those who have suffered physical abuse or molestation, those who have a history of chronic depression, teens with generally poor communication skills and teens with chronic illnesses. One retrospective study revealed that young women who had babies before the age of 17 had ten times the number of average suicide attempts.[3] Another study indicated that 1 in 12 inner-city adolescents interviewed had tried to commit suicide.[4]

Classic symptoms of depression in teenagers may include changes in eating and sleeping habits, withdrawal from friends and family and poor concentration—often manifested by a drop in school performance. Radical changes in personality and psychosomatic complaints are other frequent symptoms.[5] Older teenagers often show these symptoms; however, they may additionally show irritability, lethargy and decreased concern with their sur-

[1]"Teen Suicide Increases: Risk and Causes Identified," *American Family Physician* 36, No. 1 (July 1987): 272.
[2]Sari Staver, "Help Prevent Teen Suicides, MDs Urged," *American Medical News*, 23/30 November 1984: 39–40.
[3]Iris F. Litt, "Suicide in Adolescents," Resident and Staff Physician, July 1985, 1pc.
[4]"Teen Suicide Increases," 272.
[5]Staver, 40.

roundings, relationships, or personal hygiene.[6]

Unfortunately, not all teens demonstrate the classic warning signs of depression. Sudden rebellious behavior, truancy, multiple physical complaints, "daredevil" stunts, sexual promiscuity, frequent accidents, or a sudden frenzy of activity may all be alternative symptoms for teenage depression.[7] Signals of such depression may not be noticed unless careful attention is given to adolescent behavior changes, including seemingly blatant ones like writing about death or giving away prized possessions.

The following is just one scenario, so typical of a teenager's final plea for help:

> *No one really noticed the gradual changes in Richard, a high school student from a large, well-respected family. All of the children were bright, and Richard was one of the brightest.*
>
> *His obvious intelligence contrasted sharply with the sudden decline in his grades during his senior year. Fellow students were puzzled and concerned about laziness when his grades went from straight-A's to C's and D's. The teachers wondered why such a nice boy had suddenly chosen such a gruesome essay topic as death.*
>
> *Often a student who did not fit in with others, Richard was always gentle about the sometimes cruel teasing he received from classmates. Yet he withdrew noticeably from those few he called friends. His appearance degenerated till he looked disheveled and sloppy. People thought he either slept in his clothes—or he never slept.*
>
> *Near the end of the year, Richard suddenly seemed to develop overwhelming energy. In a frenzy of activity, he changed from taking piano lessons to trying to put together a band. When he and his classmates began receiving college acceptances, he showed none of the enthusiasm of*

---

[6]H. Norman Wright, "The Crisis of Suicide," *Crisis Counseling* (San Bernardino, Calif.: Here's Life Publishers, 1985), 106–107.

[7]American Academy of Pediatrics, Committee on Adolescence, Michael T. Cohen, Chairperson, "Teenage Suicide," *Pediatrics* 66 (July 1980), 144.

the other students, although he was accepted into a top school.

When Richard died shortly thereafter, from an "accident with a gun," surely the real accident was that no one who knew him realized the hundred subtle ways he had asked for their help.

There are no really definitive reasons "why" a teenager takes his or her own life. Often, a suicide appears to be an attempt to resolve a conflict by which the teen feels entrapped. This conflict may involve friends, parents, boyfriends or girlfriends, or even school and church groups. Personal losses, such as the death of a loved one, disruption of the family unit by divorce, or any matter that the teen perceives to be a personal, irrevocable failure, may become a precipitating event. Guilt, or fear of the consequences of such matters as legal involvements or pregnancy may again create an overwhelming conflict in an adolescent's life.[8]

Other factors that currently contribute to the escalating suicide rate must surely include media glamorization of violence and death. Teenagers may romanticize the attention or help they will receive from suicide without realizing the finality of such an act. Often teenagers are subject to strong impulse control at this stage in their lives and may impulsively take their own lives in a moment of pain, without necessarily intending a fatal outcome.[9]

Many people consider suicide, at least fleeting thoughts of it, at some painful point of their lives. Teens may commit suicide in an effort to stop emotional pain, unable to see through the moment to know they *can* survive the pain without ending their lives.

Although 5 to 8 times as many females as males attempt suicide, 4 times as many males actually commit suicide.

[8]Robert B. Shearin, "Suicide and Depression," *Adolescent Medicine* (Kalamazoo, Mich.: UpJohn Co., 1983), 131.
[9]American Academy of Pediatrics, "Teenage Suicide," 144.

These statistics probably reflect the more lethal methods males choose, including firearms and hanging as compared to medication overdoses, which are the most common method attempted by females.[10] Many actual suicide attempts by adolescents are fraught with mixed feelings— struggling between a wish to die and a hope of rescue. Therefore, they can give off incongruent signals: While they may try to take their lives by highly lethal means, they may also offer many advance warning signals in the hope of being discovered and rescued in time.[11]

The key to prevention of teen suicides is to alert and mobilize parents, teachers, friends, health personnel and other potential rescuers, teaching them to recognize high-risk teens, or behavioral clues preceding a suicide attempt and how to intervene.[12] Surprisingly, an estimated 80 percent of suicide victims mention their intent before their attempts.[13]

Of course, any non-suicidal adolescent may have some of the same behavior characteristics as one contemplating suicide. Therefore, we must ask in order to know. Remember that thoughts of suicide need to be brought into the open for you to be able to help. Asking about suicide will not plant the idea of suicide in the mind of someone who is not already contemplating it. It will often offer the relief of being able to talk about it to someone who *is* thinking about it. Take a supportive attitude and encourage a young person; that's the best first step. Remember that people contemplating suicide are usually ambivalent about living or dying.[14] Therefore, they need suggestions of hope, and the support of someone who will point out reasons to live.

If you suspect an adolescent is suicidal, maintain fre-

---

[10]"Teenage Suicide," 144.
[11]Leon Eisenberg, "Adolescent Suicide: On Taking Arms Against a Sea of Troubles," *Pediatrics* 66 (July 1980), 319.
[12]Staver, 39.
[13]Wright, 100.
[14]Eisenberg, 319.

quent and open contact. Encourage them to call or to stop by in person. Listen to everything they have to say—and then offer hope. For example, "I'm glad we can talk about this," and "I believe there is help for you." Try to pinpoint the problems and listen to the story, his or her previous attempts to cope and what the current problem is. Try to focus on his or her feelings and try not to moralize. Exploring his reasons for wanting to die can help to break up feelings of overwhelming helplessness into more manageable portions.[15]

Referral to professionals trained in intervention is a wise course of action. Professional intervention will include assessment of the teenager's risk of suicide and treatment, help through counseling, and possibly medication. A teen may be treated as an outpatient or during hospitalization, according to the assessed danger. Important aspects of any treatment include mobilizing family support for therapy, discussion and increasing observation of the patient.[16] The patient's home must be cleared of any potentially lethal weapons.[17] The counselor may ask the patient and family to initiate a "contract" to assure the patient's safety during the time of healing. Friends who offer acceptance and support are also of major importance.

Some mistaken ideas about suicide include:

1. *"People who talk about suicide don't do it."* Remember—80 percent of those who commit suicide have communicated their intent previously.
2. *"Suicide is only a danger in certain classes or ages."* No—suicide crosses all ages and classes.[18]
3. *"Improvement after depression means the risk has passed."* Fifty percent of suicides occur within three months of the first crisis.

[15]Wright, 108–110.
[16]Shearin, 130–131.
[17]Eisenberg, 317.
[18]Jerry Johnston, *Why Suicide?* (Nashville: Oliver-Nelson Books, 1987), 135–137.

4. *"Christians don't commit suicide."* Christians are still human—subject to emotional pain and problems in life.[19]

What else can be done? The number of susceptible teens is now higher than ever before, due to rampant alcohol and drug abuse, broken homes and the glamorization of violence on television and in movies—in addition to the usual pressures of adolescence, including sexual activity and peer pressure. For society to restore the "taboo" against suicide rather than to contribute to these factors would help, as would removal of easy access to lethal weapons.[20]

One unique problem with teen suicides is their tendency to "cluster." After one teenage suicide, multiple suicides tend to follow in the same area in rapid sequence. If the first teen was popular, his or her death tends to be romanticized by teens and may spur a rash of similar deaths. For example, in 1983 eight teenagers took their lives in a Dallas suburb within three months;[21] in another Texas city in early 1984, six teens took their lives. Across the continent, ten New York teens in Westchester took their lives over an eight-month period.[22] We must, therefore, emphasize to teens the hope of living and minimize associated sensationalism of death by suicide.

The epidemic of teenage suicides in the United States destroys not only the lives and future potential of approximately 5,400 teenagers each year, but it tragically ravages the lives of their friends and families after their deaths.[23] I was reminded of this fact while talking with a beautiful high school student who had been very close to her

---

[19]Wright, 100–101.
[20]Eisenberg, 319.
[21]Michael Doan, "As 'Cluster Suicides' Take Toll of Teenagers," with Sarah Peterson, *U.S. News & World Report*, 12 November 1984, 499–550.
[22]Staver, 39.
[23]National Center for Health Statistics: Advance Report of Final Mortality Statistics, 1985, *Monthly Vital Statistics Report*, 28 August 1987, 20.

brother. In the two years following his death by suicide, she had managed to struggle through her own numbness and her friends' awkwardness to achieve high grades, a college scholarship and get elected to an office of popularity in her school. However, through her sobbing and heartache, she told me she would trade it all for one more day of laughter with her brother.

We can look at all the statistics we want, and still miss one of the most important facts about suicide. It is not a lone act. Suicide mars—even ruins—the lives of many, many people.

Linda Beahm, M.D.
Family Practice

A Note From Donalyn

I am always encour-
aged when people tell me
that they have been
blessed by hearing how the Lord has worked in my life.

If you would like to let me know how the Lord has
carried you through a difficult time or how this book has
touched your heart, I would like to hear from you. If you
would like an answer too, please include a self-addressed
stamped envelope.

I also enjoy meeting new friends and visiting places I
have never had the opportunity to see. If you would like
to have me as a guest speaker in your church or organi-
zation, feel free to contact me.

Remember that the Lord has a wonderful plan for your
life. His reasons go beyond our own. He gives us all a
reason to live.

Donalyn Powell
Sunnylake Farm
Route 4, Box 343
Rustburg, VA 24588

Bibliography

American Academy of Pediatrics, Committee on Adolescence, Michael I. Cohen, Chairperson. "Teenage Suicide." Pediatrics 66 (July 1980), 144–146.

Doan, Michael. "As 'Cluster Suicides' Take Toll on Teenagers" with Sarah Peterson. U.S. News & World Report, 12 November 1984, 49–50.

Eisenberg, Leon. "Adolescent Suicide: On Taking Arms Against a Sea of Troubles." Pediatrics 66 (July 1980), 315–320.

Johnston, Jerry. Why Suicide? Nashville, Tenn.: Oliver-Nelson Books, 1987.

Litt, Iris F. "Suicide in Adolescence." Resident & Staff Physician (July 1986), 1pc–3pc.

National Center for Health Statistics: Advance Report of Final Mortality Statistics, 1985. Monthly Vital Statistics Report Vol. 36, No. 5, Supp. DHHS Pub. No. (PHS) 87–1120. Public Health Service. Hyattsville, Md., 28 August 1987.

Shearin, Robert B. "Suicide and Depression." Adolescent Medicine, Kalamazoo, Mich.: UpJohn Co., 1983.

Staver, Sari. "Help Prevent Teen Suicides, MDs Urged." American Family Physician vol. 36, No. 1 (July 1987), 272–275.

Wright, H. Norman. Crisis Counseling. San Bernardino, Calif.: Here's Life Publishers, 1985.